THE FINAL TEST

THE FINAL TEST
by Chris Paling

JOSEF WEINBERGER PLAYS

LONDON

THE FINAL TEST
First published in 2013
by Josef Weinberger Ltd
12-14 Mortimer Street, London W1T 3JJ
www.josef-weinberger.com / plays@jwmail.co.uk

ISBN: 978 0 85676 329 8

Printed by Commercial Colour Press plc, Hainault, Essex

For my father

THE FINAL TEST was first presented by Ian Dickens Productions
International Ltd at Lincoln Theatre Royal on 6th June 2012
prior to a national tour. The cast was as follows:

PETER	Colin Baker
RUTH	Karen Ford
SUSAN	Helena Waite-Roberts
RAY	Peter Amory
POLICEMAN	Michael Garland
REMOVAL MAN	Gavin Kerr

The role of SUSAN was played by Nicola Weeks during the
national tour.

Directed by Ian Dickens

Set design by Alan Miller Bunford

Sound and lighting design by Steve Chambers

Associate Producer Brian Daniels

CHARACTERS

PETER

RUTH, PETER'S wife

RAY

SUSAN, RAY'S wife

A POLICEMAN

A REMOVAL MAN

The action takes place over the course of a five day test match in the garden and kitchen/dining room of a detached house in the present day.

ACT ONE

Scene One

*A suburban garden. Day. A late middle-aged man – PETER,
early/late 60s – is in a deckchair on his lawn. A large sheet
of newspaper (The Daily Telegraph) is draped over his head
to shield him from the high mid-day sun. It rises and falls as
he breathes, deep in sleep. We hear the sound of a test match
cricket commentary from a portable radio by his side, next
to a large glass of orange juice. (Alternatively, PETER can be
listening to the commentary by an earpiece connected to a
radio, however the commentary must be audible as the scene
begins and can then fade out).*

The next door garden is shielded by a high hedge.

*To the right of him, slanted across the stage, large French
doors face onto a patio. This is a substantial house. On left
of stage there is a small shed. There should be a sense of the
garden continuing beyond the left boundary of the stage.*

A MAN *in a brown, three-quarter length coat approaches
through the French doors and stands, hands in pockets,
enjoying the sun on his face for a while.*

He looks towards PETER *and addresses him.*

MAN	We're done.
	(No response from PETER. *The paper rises and falls.)*
MAN	Yes. We're all loaded up.
	(No response from PETER. *The* MAN *coughs to gain his attention.* PETER *wakes and removes the paper. Looks at the man without recognition or understanding.)*
MAN	Sorry to wake you.

PETER   That's quite all right. I was just . . . listening
                 to the cricket. The final test. From The Oval.

MAN   We've finished.

PETER   Have you?

MAN   Yes. All packed and ready to go.

PETER   (*slightly confused*) Oh Good . . . Well done.

MAN   What about the deckchair?

PETER   What about it?

MAN   Is it staying or going?

PETER   This deckchair?

MAN   Yes.

PETER   Well it's staying.

MAN   And the radio?

PETER   That's staying too. And the . . . (*Picks up
                 glass.*) ah, orange juice. In fact everything in
                 the garden is staying: the lawn, the hedge . . .

MAN   The shed?

PETER   Oh yes. The shed definitely remains. As does
                 the path and the vegetable patch.

MAN   Righty ho.

PETER   Righty ho then.

MAN   See you at the other end.

PETER   Yes.

                   (*The man walks off through the windows.*
                   PETER *watches him go with some bemusement.*)

PETER   . . . Or possibly no. Extraordinary man.

                   (*He picks up the sheet of newspaper and
                   reads it. The commentary continues. It's the
                   only sound we can hear except for a buzzing
                   bee. A woman – RUTH – slightly younger
                   and less worn than PETER, comes to stand at
                   the threshold of the house. She is wearing a
                   light summer dress and has a light mac over
                   her arm. She looks out at PETER with some
                   curiosity, but without much fondness. She
                   emerges.*)

RUTH   How are they doing?

PETER   Thirty-five for two.

RUTH   Oh good.

PETER   No. It's not good at all.

RUTH   Isn't it?

PETER   No. They've scored thirty-five runs for the
                   loss of two wickets.

RUTH   So they've run up and down the pitch
                   thirty-five times in this heat. That should be
                   applauded, shouldn't it?

PETER   It's their job.

RUTH   Even so, in this heat . . . I was watching you.

PETER   Were you?

RUTH   Yes. From the bedroom window.

PETER   And what did you see?

RUTH   Nothing unexpected.

PETER   Well, I'm sorry about that I really am but it's
                a bit hot to do anything unexpected.

RUTH   Don't apologise. I think it would have
                shocked me if I had seen anything
                unexpected. It might have changed my mind.

PETER   About what?

RUTH   Oh, I don't know. Perhaps you should hazard
                a guess.

                (*Now she comes closer and looks up at the
                sun.*)

PETER   I'm listening to the final test. Well, trying
                despite constant interruptions . . . I don't
                have time to hazard guesses.

RUTH   Can't you hazard and listen at the same time?

PETER   I doubt it. Though I've never tried.

RUTH   Try.

PETER   (*he considers the proposition*) No. Nothing,
                I'm afraid.

RUTH   The silly game goes on for three weeks.
                There's surely plenty of time to do other
                things.

PETER   The game goes on for five days. The series
                lasts three weeks.

RUTH	Well it feels like three weeks. Silly men running around in white clothes to no avail.
PETER	They're not silly and it's not to no avail – it's cricket. Cricket is all avail.
RUTH	Anyway, it seems like a waste of a perfectly good playing field to me.
PETER	Test matches?
RUTH	Cricket in general. It takes up far too much room.
PETER	Not as much as golf.
RUTH	No, I'll grant you that, but golf doesn't take over huge swathes of cities.
PETER	No. It takes over even huger swathes of the countryside. So I can't say I agree, but you're welcome to your opinion.
RUTH	Thank you. That's good of you.
PETER	Not at all.

(*Now he notices she's dressed to go out.*)

| PETER | Are you going out? |
| RUTH | In a manner of speaking. |

(PETER *thinks about this for a moment.*)

PETER	'In a manner of speaking'?
RUTH	Yes.
PETER	That sounds a bit . . . obfuscatory.

RUTH	I suppose it is.
PETER	I mean you're either going out or you're not. Simple as that.
RUTH	Oh, I am going out.
PETER	Well there you are then.
RUTH	But simply 'going out' would imply, in some way, that one was returning.
PETER	Yes. It would. I'll grant you that.
RUTH	Peter . . .
PETER	Yes, Ruth?
RUTH	You know I love you.
PETER	Yes. And I love you. Always have. Always will. You know that.
RUTH	Yes, I do know that, which makes this all very . . .

(*A wicket on the commentary.*)

PETER	Just a minute!
RUTH	What?
PETER	Another wicket. Complete collapse. They'll have us all out before we've reached 100.
RUTH	You see this is exactly the problem.
PETER	Yes. It is. We have no openers worth their salt.
RUTH	I'm not talking about openers. I'm talking about us.

PETER   Well, forgive me, darling, but I doubt either you or I are of an age to be capable of facing that kind of hostile quick bowling.

RUTH   I sometimes wonder if you say things like that just to make me angry.

PETER   Of course I don't.

RUTH   Then maybe that's worse. You simply don't . . . connect.

PETER   With you?

RUTH   With anybody.

PETER   I connect with all kinds of people. It was my job.

RUTH   Your job was to manage people. Not connect with them.

PETER   Are you having an off day, darling?

RUTH   (*sighs hard*) No. I'm not having an off day.

PETER   Would you like me to fetch you a drink?

RUTH   No. Well yes. But in a moment. There's something we need to talk about first.

PETER   That sounds rather serious. (*He sits up a bit.*) Shall I fetch the other deck chair out of the shed? If we're going to have a serious talk, I mean.

RUTH   No. I'd prefer to stand.

PETER   Oh. Well should I stand up too? Is it going to be that kind of conversation?

RUTH	No. Not necessary . . . What kind of conversation?
PETER	I'm sorry?
RUTH	I'm just intrigued to know what kind of conversation you imagine would entail two people having to stand up.
PETER	Ah.
RUTH	Rather than one standing and one sitting.
PETER	To be quite honest I think I'd have trouble defining exactly what kind of conversation that was – although two people standing would denote a certain degree of formality, wouldn't it?
RUTH	Or informality. A party, for example.
PETER	Yes. You're right. I mean if you enter a room in which a party is taking place and a couple of people are seated they do tend to rise to greet you, don't they?
RUTH	Yes.
PETER	So, although it's an informal setting, there is a certain degree of formality required. Although . . . although, say you were to re-enter the room a second time, and, just say for sake of argument, those same two people had returned to the sofa, it's unlikely that they'd get up again.
RUTH	Unless new guests arrived.
PETER	Yes. Of course. So there we are. Let off the social hook. Conundrum solved.

(PETER *settles back*.)

RUTH	But that's not what I wanted to talk to you about.
PETER	Isn't it?
RUTH	You're very good at changing the subject.
PETER	Well thank you.
RUTH	That wasn't a compliment.
PETER	Well do you mind if I take it as one?
RUTH	Peter. Please. Let me . . . There's something I need to talk to you about.
PETER	Right. Well in that case I insist on fetching you a drink. It's much too hot for you to be standing there speaking seriously without any means of hydration.
RUTH	(*exasperated*) Oh. All right.
PETER	Orange juice do you?
RUTH	Yes. Anything.

(*He stands and sets off for the house. Then pauses.*)

PETER	Bits or no bits?
RUTH	What?
PETER	Orange juice. Bits or no bits?
RUTH	I really don't care.

PETER   I'll get you the expensive stuff then, with the
               bits. (*A few more steps. Then he stops.*) It is
               odd isn't it?

RUTH   What?

PETER   Well normally one pays more for
               unadulterated food items. Orange juice is the
               exception isn't it? I can't think of any other
               examples, can you?

RUTH   Peter. I really don't have time for this.

PETER   Right. Well, stay there and I'll fetch it. Take
               the deck chair.

               (PETER *goes into the house.* RUTH *shakes her
               head in some despair, wanders to the hedge,
               looks over, then returns to the chair, but
               doesn't sit. A moment.* PETER *dashes out.*)

PETER   I think you better had sit down.

RUTH   Why?

PETER   I have some rather bad news.

RUTH   I'll stay standing if you don't mind.

PETER   Are you sure?

RUTH   Peter. Please. Just say it.

PETER   We've been robbed!

RUTH   I don't think so.

PETER   No? Well, prepare yourself for a shock: there
               is no furniture whatsoever on the ground
               floor of the house.

RUTH   Did you look upstairs too?

PETER   No. My God, do you think they cleared the whole house?

RUTH   Yes.

              (PETER *dashes back in. A pause.*)

PETER   (*off*) You're absolutely right!

              (RUTH *looks behind her. No* PETER.)

RUTH   Where are you?

PETER   (*off*) Up here.

              (RUTH *looks up to the first floor.*)

RUTH   Well?

PETER   (*off*) Everything's gone.

RUTH   I told you.

PETER   (*off*) But they must have been quick . . . And very silent. I mean surely you were in the house all the time.

RUTH   I was, yes. Come down, Peter, I'm getting a crick in my neck.

PETER   (*off*) Righty ho.

              (*A pause.* PETER *enters.*)

PETER   You didn't notice all of our possessions being stolen?

RUTH   No.

PETER   They drugged you? Of course. They drugged
             you. That's why you're in such an odd frame
             of mind.

RUTH   We weren't robbed, Peter.

PETER   No?

RUTH   No.

PETER   Then . . . You gave it away to charity?

RUTH   No, Peter. I gave money to the drought
             appeal. I don't think they'd have had much
             use for your trouser press on the African
             plains.

PETER   Then the furniture was removed by
             somebody who . . . ? Sorry, just trying to
             puzzle this through. Somebody who had your
             permission?

RUTH   Correct.

PETER   Ah! There was a man – a man in a brown
             coat – came out to talk to me a while ago
             about being packed and ready to go.

RUTH   Yes. That's right. And do you remember
             I told you I was watching you from the
             bedroom window?

PETER   I remember that.

RUTH   You see, I thought . . . I thought I'll give
             him one more chance. One more chance to
             do something normal. To respond in a way
             a normal human being might respond when,
             say, a complete stranger comes into his
             garden uninvited and tells you he's loaded
             up. But you didn't even turn a hair.

PETER   I was listening to the test!

RUTH   Listening to cricket on the radio doesn't make
               the rest of your brain go to mush, does it?

PETER   Not entirely, no. But it does involve some
               concentration.

PETER   I mean you need to allow the picture to be
               built in your head, otherwise you might as
               well watch it on the television with all those
               ridiculous diagrammes and hotspots and
               graphics. Cricket shouldn't be about graphs.
               It's about life . . .

RUTH   Peter.

PETER   . . . the whole gamut of human emotion:
               an opera in three acts played out on a
               beautifully tailored greensward, a thousand
               moments of tension and release, tension, and
               release . . .

RUTH   Peter.

PETER   . . . the fast bowler steaming in, smoke
               snorting from his nostrils, from the pavilion
               end while the batsman looks on impassively.
               HOWZAT! . . .

RUTH   Peter I'm leaving you.

               (*She turns and moves to the door. Silence but
               for the commentary from the game.*)

PETER   You're . . .

RUTH   Leaving you.

PETER   Ah.

RUTH	'Ah'. Yes, well that just about sums it up really, doesn't it?
PETER	When?
RUTH	When?
PETER	Yes.
RUTH	Wouldn't a more appropriate question be why?
PETER	Yes. I was coming to that one.
RUTH	Well why did you ask when I was leaving?
PETER	Because I have to know how much time I've got. I mean if you'd said "Now, this very minute," then I'd have known I had very little time to understand why, whereas if you'd said tomorrow, or next week, or next year then we'd have had plenty of time to get to the bottom of things.
RUTH	Soon. I'm leaving very soon.
PETER	And where are you going?
RUTH	Bexhill-on-Sea.
PETER	Bexhill-on-Sea! But that's miles away. How many miles?
RUTH	Ninety-seven miles to be exact. According to the internet route planner.
PETER	Did you check?
RUTH	Yes.
PETER	Why?

RUTH	Shall I tell you why? Do you really want to know?
PETER	Yes.
RUTH	Because I knew that was another stupid question you were going to ask me.
PETER	Well it seems a perfectly reasonable question for a man to ask of his wife when she tells him she's leaving him.
RUTH	Why?
PETER	Because he has to plan how many stops he's going to need when he visits her. How many tanks of petrol, for example. Will he need to fill up before he leaves and if he does, does that mean he'll not have to fill up again until his return?
RUTH	And the fact that you think it is a reasonable question is exactly why I'm leaving you. Because, and I'll be perfectly honest now, I was beginning to doubt my sanity.
PETER	Oh dear.
RUTH	Yes. I was beginning to wonder if I was the one who was being unreasonable, not you. But then, after several months of fairly intense soul searching with a therapist, I have concluded that I am normal – and sane – and you are not.
PETER	You've seen a therapist? Good grief. I didn't know you were mentally unstable.
RUTH	I'm not. I'm extremely stable. That's what he taught me.

PETER   Is he qualified to make such a judgement?

RUTH   Yes. Simon has several certificates on his
               wall.

PETER   They could have been fakes.

RUTH   They were not fakes.

PETER   Were they watermarked? Did you check? Did
               you ring the institutions which awarded them
               and ask whether the young man in question
               actually attended?

RUTH   No. I had no reason to. And why do you
               assume he's a young man?

PETER   Simon: It's a young man's name.

RUTH   Is it?

PETER   Yes. Well in that case I think you might find
               you've been adjudged stable by somebody
               not competent to do so.

               (RUTH *breathes hard.*)

RUTH   Peter. I'm not going to get angry. This is not
               the time. I'm beyond anger and into the . . .
               (*Breathes deeply.*) calm waters of rational
               thought.

PETER   I beg to differ on that one.

RUTH   Differ all you like.

PETER   And what are you going to do in Bexhill-
               on-Sea? You can't spend your entire life
               wandering around the De La Warr Pavilion
               you know.

RUTH	I'm going to walk on the seafront with Steven.
PETER	Winter and summer?
RUTH	Both. And we're going to swim in the sea, even on winter days, possibly without benefit of costumes, and we're going to take several holidays a year – short ones to places of artistic merit – with like minded people, who we will converse with in a civilised, normal fashion. And we will go on the occasional cruise. And I've signed up for a watercolour class and a poetry course.
PETER	Poetry? At your age?
RUTH	Yes.
PETER	Your father will turn in his grave to learn there's a poet in the family.
RUTH	Please . . .
PETER	And a cruise! You don't like cruise ships.
	(RUTH *shakes her head.*)
PETER	What?
RUTH	It's you who doesn't like cruise ships. I have never been on one.
PETER	Well there you are. I assure you you'll come down with the norovirus within 24 hours of embarking. It's virtually guaranteed in the brochures.
RUTH	And Steven?

PETER   Yes. Steven too. Unless he has a cast iron
               constitution. Which I doubt, given his
               profession.

RUTH   You don't know what his profession is.

PETER   Therapist.

RUTH   He's not a therapist.

PETER   You said he was.

RUTH   No. I said I was seeing a therapist whose
               name is Simon. I met Steven separately. On
               the internet.

PETER   Ah.

RUTH   What's that supposed to mean?

PETER   Forgive me, my darling, but I think you'll
               find that this adonis you imagine you've
               been speaking to on the internet is actually a
               twenty-five stone lorry driver from Thurrock
               with halitosis.

RUTH   He's not.

PETER   You've met him?

RUTH   Of course I've met him. You don't think I'd
               move to Bexhill-on-Sea with somebody I
               hadn't met before?

PETER   I don't know. I really don't. I do not
               recognise the woman I married: all this talk
               of cruises and Bexhill-on-Sea and frolicking
               naked in the waves. I mean – It's . . . barely
               credible.

RUTH   So you're not curious about Steven?

PETER	Should I be?
RUTH	I'm leaving you for another man and you're not curious to know anything about him – beyond some ludicrous assumptions?
PETER	. . . Well . . . Well, yes, I suppose. I suppose I am curious about him.
RUTH	You can ask me anything you like. Anything at all. I want us to be as open as possible.
PETER	All right . . . All right . . .
RUTH	We need to make this work, Peter. We've been married for thirty-five years. I want us to stay friends.
PETER	Well let us begin by getting one thing straight: I absolutely refuse to accompany you and Steven on a cruise ship.
RUTH	(*irony*) In which case I'll make sure we don't accidentally book you a ticket.
PETER	Good. And I absolutely will not be swimming without my trunks on – winter or summer.
RUTH	So, anything else? Ask away. Anything you like. Anything at all.
PETER	What size shoes does he wear?
	(*Exasperated*, RUTH *goes to the French doors.*)
RUTH	Do you do this on purpose?
PETER	What?

(*She becomes clinically practical.*)

RUTH   Right. A couple of practical details before I
            leave.

PETER   Yes?

RUTH   There are two suitcases of your clothes and
            things in the dining room. The house has
            been sold.

PETER   What? I don't remember selling the house.

RUTH   You signed the contract last week without
            looking at it and several other documents
            previously in the same fashion. We complete
            on the sale in approximately five minutes.
            Your half of the furniture is in storage.
            Here are the details. (*She hands him a slip
            of paper.*) Your share of the proceeds from
            the house will be transferred into our joint
            deposit account, which is now solely your
            account, on completion. I have also removed
            my name from the joint current account and
            set up one in my name. Should you wish to
            contact me you can reach me on my mobile
            phone, by e-mail or through my Facebook
            page.

PETER   What in God's name is a Facebook page?

RUTH   It's a personal advertising hoarding on the
            internet on which you post details about the
            full life you are leading. Or, in my case, the
            full life I intend to leave when I walk out
            through that door.

PETER   I see.

RUTH   I may even take up blogging.

PETER   What, with your back?

RUTH   Blogging – it's a method of communication
            in which people reveal short, regular titbits
            about their lives to interested parties.

PETER   Why on earth should anyone be interested in
            titbits? What happened to privacy?

RUTH   It's how the modern world works, Peter.
            Privacy has gone public.

PETER   Well I want no part of it.

RUTH   You have no part of it.

PETER   Good. Then so shall it remain.

RUTH   This might seem cruel, Peter. It might seem
            heartless and callous. But I have not done
            this lightly, nor have I done it solely for
            my benefit. I have done it to shake you up
            and in an attempt to make you connect in
            a reasonably conventional way with other
            members of the human race – something
            which you have signally failed to do for the
            last sixty-three years of your life. Goodbye,
            Peter.

PETER   But who will I do the crossword with?

RUTH   You'll find somebody else. I'm sure you'd
            be considered quite a catch.

PETER   I'm too old to be hanging round
            discotheques in cravats.

RUTH   There are other ways of meeting members
            of the opposite sex nowadays that don't
            involve cravats. Besides, you'll have my
            phone number and if you get stuck with the
            crossword you can call.

PETER	. . . This Steven character.
RUTH	Yes.
PETER	How old is he?
RUTH	Forty-three.

(PETER *nods*.)

PETER	And what is his profession?
RUTH	He's between jobs – he taught. I think. EFL. But he intends to work again.
PETER	Good.

(RUTH *nods*.)

PETER	And he . . . he'll be good to you.
RUTH	I don't need someone to be good to me. You're as good a man as I've ever met. I need to be loved.

(*She dashes back and kisses him on the cheek. She looks at him. They look at each other. For a moment they both acknowledge the seriousness of this. She sniffs back a tear.*)

PETER	So the house has been sold?
RUTH	Yes.
PETER	Where will I live?

(RUTH *regains her composure*.)

RUTH	The decision is yours. It will be the first step you'll have to take on your own.

PETER	Nobody can force me to leave my own home.
RUTH	Indeed not. But, as I said, this is no longer your own home. Goodbye.

(*She composes herself, turns heel and walks out. A pause.* PETER *wanders towards the deck chair with his hands in his pockets. Just the commentary on the radio.*)

PETER	Bexhill-on-Sea . . .

(*A wicket falls. He sits heavily in the chair and leans towards the radio.*)

PETER	Collapse. They're collapsing. . .

(*Blackout. The scene change is bridged by the sound of cricket commentary. It fades beneath.*)

Scene Two

Mid-afternoon. PETER *has his two suitcases beside his deck chair. He continues to listen to the cricket on the radio. Distant sound of a lorry backing. Air brakes. Doors open and slam. Voices.* PETER *stiffens and responds with a brief turn of his head towards the house. He steels himself, sits up a little straighter, goes on listening to the radio.*

Sound of a young woman and man, off. SUSAN'S *accent is resolutely middle class –* RAY *is a rough diamond.*

SUSAN	(*off*) Well come on!
RAY	(*off*) I can't.
SUSAN	(*off*) Yes you can. It's romantic. Carry me over the threshold.

RAY   (*off*) I've got a bad back. You'll have to wait
               for romance until my back's better.

SUSAN   (*off*) Don't be so miserable.

RAY   (*off*) I'm miserable because my back's bad.

SUSAN   (*off*) Oh, get over yourself. Lift me up.

               (*Pause.*)

RAY   (*off*) Ouch!

SUSAN   (*off*) Oh never mind.

RAY   (*off*) No. Let me try.

SUSAN   (*off*) I don't want to make it any worse.

RAY   (*off*) Give me a minute to get my breath
               back.

SUSAN   (*off*) Oh, never mind. The moment's passed.

               (*Pause.*)

SUSAN   (*off, approaching through the house*) Oh,
               look, they left the French windows open.

RAY   (*off*) That was a bit stupid of them. We could
               have had squatters.

               (SUSAN – *late 20s, blonde, light summer
               dress – appears at the French window.*)

SUSAN   It's a lovely garden though. Really well
               tende . . .

               (*Now her gaze takes in* PETER. *A double take.*
               PETER *does not turn.*)

RAY	(*still off*) They've cleaned it up though. The place is spotless.
SUSAN	(*fierce whisper*) Ray.
RAY	(*off*) And they've left the curtains. Did we pay for them? I hope not. They're horrible.
SUSAN	Ray!
RAY	(*off*) What?
SUSAN	(*sharper whisper*) Ray!
RAY	(*off*) What?
SUSAN	Come here.

(RAY *appears in t-shirt and shorts – similar age to* SUSAN. *He is holding his back. He sees* PETER. *They mime a "what's he doing here?" "Who is he?" conversation.* SUSAN *then pushes* RAY *out towards* PETER *to confront him.* RAY *is embarrassed, and moves to stand over* PETER, *hands in pockets, as if they are meeting at a social gathering.* SUSAN *remains on the patio by the French doors.* RAY *winces a smile at* PETER. PETER *returns it. During the following,* SUSAN *becomes increasingly annoyed at the way the conversation progresses.*)

RAY	Hello.
PETER	Hello.
RAY	. . . Fantastic day.
PETER	Indeed. I understand we're expected to wear cream nowadays whenever we step outside

in the summer. But it seems unnecessary to
me. Do you wear cream?

RAY   Yes.

PETER   Really?

RAY   Yes. Factor 15. I burn easy.

PETER   Yes, you're quite pale-skinned, aren't you?

RAY   Yes. And it tends to get me on the top of the
                 legs. Just above the knees.

                 (PETER *looks.*)

PETER   Oh yes, I can see the slight redness. Have
                 you been out in it this morning?

RAY   Yes. When we were loading the van.

PETER   You missed the mid-day sun then. I
                 understand that's the worst.

RAY   I imagine the NHS will start imposing
                 curfews soon to prevent people venturing out
                 in it.

                 (SUSAN *shakes her head with annoyance.*
                 PETER *looks at his knees.*)

PETER   I don't wear shorts. At my age I think it
                 would be considered to be some kind of
                 crime. I'd be had up for indecency.

RAY   I'm sure you've got decent legs.

PETER   Oh I used to have. In my twenties I was
                 forever displaying them on the tennis courts.
                 Alas, no longer.

(RAY *looks towards* SUSAN *and shrugs. She looks daggers back – mimes, "Tell him to go!" Pause. Commentary continues.*)

RAY   How are they doing?

PETER   Well they haven't lost any wickets for a couple of hours. Plodding on. Digging in.

RAY   Good . . . Good.

                 (*Now he looks sheepishly to* SUSAN *and shrugs again.* SUSAN *shakes her head, crosses her arms and stalks over to join them, looking daggers at* RAY.)

SUSAN   (*cold*) Hello.

PETER   Oh, hello. Now I expect you do wear sun cream. Women tend to be better organized in that respect.

                 (*He turns to* RAY, *who nods agreement.*)

SUSAN   I wonder if you'd be kind enough to explain exactly what you're doing in our garden.

PETER   Yes, I was afraid that was going to come up sooner or later.

SUSAN   Well?

PETER   You see, the fact is, I live here.

SUSAN   (*some relief*) Oh. You're Mr Rattenbury!

PETER   That's right.

SUSAN   It's Mr Rattenbury, Ray.

RAY   (*smiles*) Oh, Mr Rattenbury. Nice to meet
               you.

PETER   And you too.

               (PETER *stands. They shake hands politely.*)

SUSAN   (*softens*) I only had dealings with your wife.
               She said you were away most of the time.

PETER   Yes, I bet she did.

SUSAN   So did you not hear from your solicitor?

PETER   No, my wife was dealing with all that
               apparently.

SUSAN   Well we've completed on the sale. And I can
               see you've moved your stuff out. So . . .

               (*She looks at* RAY.)

RAY   . . . So I expect we'd better get on with
               moving in and let you get on with moving in
               to your new place.

               (*Turns to* SUSAN.)

SUSAN   . . . Yes, we'll leave you to collect your
               belongings and . . .

RAY   . . . And wish you all the best in your new
               home.

SUSAN   Yes.

RAY   And nice to meet you . . . At last.

PETER   And you too.

(Susan *smiles.* Ray *smiles. Job done. She*
leads the way back into the house. Another
smile from Ray, *then he follows.* Peter
settles back into his chair. Slow fade out.
Again commentary peaks, bridges the
change,and fades under.)

Scene Three

The garden, early evening. Peter *remains in his chair.*
The sun is lower. On the cricket commentary we hear the
declaration that the day's play is over and stumps have been
drawn.

Through the French doors which are now closed, we can see
Susan *watching.*

Peter *stands and stretches. He turns. Sees* Susan *and waves.*
She doesn't return his wave, but stalks away into the interior
of the house, out of sight.

PETER   Well . . . Well, well, well.

               (*He kneels down on aged knees and opens*
               his suitcase. From it he takes out a pile of
               shirts, a set of braces, some underpants,
               socks, pyjamas, and a cricketing cap, which
               he looks at fondly, then puts on. He opens
               the other suitcase and finds in it a silver foil
               package which he opens: sandwiches. And a
               thermos.)

PETER   Good girl. Good girl.

               (*He pours out a cup of tea and takes a sip.*
               He then puts the cup on the ground and
               heads over to the shed. He opens the door
               and goes in. He emerges with a large garden
               umbrella and a stand which he carries over
               to his deck chair and puts up, affording the
               chair complete cover.)

(SUSAN, *followed by* RAY, *returns to the*
window and watches PETER'S *antics with*
increasing annoyance. Over the following he
potters back and forth to the shed, fetching
various things: a Calor Gas light, a small
trestle table, a tarpaulin, a rug, a waxed
coat, a cardboard box of wine.)

SUSAN   You'll have to say something.

RAY   What?

SUSAN   How about, "get out of our garden you daft
          old sod, you don't live here any more."

RAY   That's a bit strong isn't it?

SUSAN   I don't care how you put it. We can't have
          him staying out there all night – or even
          longer. He'll be wanting to use the toilet
          next.

RAY   Unless he goes in the shed.

SUSAN   I don't want him using our shed for his
          deposits.

RAY   Well make your mind up – either he uses the
          shed or you let him in to use the toilet.

SUSAN   Or he just leaves and uses somebody else's
          toilet.

          (*Pause.*)

RAY   You'd think his wife would have missed him
          by now.

SUSAN   Unless she left him here on purpose.

RAY	That's a thought. Did you check the small print on the fixtures and fittings?
SUSAN	Why?
RAY	(*smiles*) Well maybe he was included: one garden shed, one daft old sod.
	(SUSAN *looks at him – she doesn't enjoy the joke.*)
SUSAN	I'm glad you find this funny, Ray, because I don't.
	(RAY *loses the smile from his face.*)
SUSAN	You like him, don't you?
RAY	He seems all right.
SUSAN	He's a menace. I know his type.
RAY	And what type is that?
SUSAN	Helpless victims.
RAY	He seems a pretty decent old codger to me.
SUSAN	If he had any shred of decency in him he'd leave.
RAY	Perhaps he's had some kind of breakdown.
	(SUSAN *gives it some thought.*)
SUSAN	Yes. Well I suppose sometimes people can't accept change. You know, like your father when you put him in that nursing home. He hated it.

RAY	When we put him in that nursing home, Susan. He didn't want to leave his own home. That's why he hated it.
SUSAN	But it was for his own good.
RAY	So you said.
SUSAN	You were the one who said you didn't want him living with us.
RAY	Because it wouldn't have worked.
SUSAN	Should I call his wife? I've got her mobile somewhere.
RAY	Good idea.
	(*She goes off.*)
RAY	(*to himself*) . . . Didn't hate it for long, did he? Three months he lasted in there. Three months . . .
	(RAY *continues watching* PETER. *Now we're back with* PETER *who has arranged himself quite comfortably in the garden. He looks round in a contented way, sees* RAY *watching, and waves companionably.* RAY, *sheepishly, looks behind him to check* SUSAN *hasn't seen, and waves back.*)
PETER	(*calls*) Lovely evening!
RAY	Yes.
PETER	Did you hear the close of play?
RAY	No.
PETER	229 for 5.

RAY   Oh dear.

PETER   Yes. Poor. But something of a comeback . . .
               Are you settling in all right?

RAY   Fine.

PETER   Just between you and me, I'm not a great fan
               of those curtains myself. I won't be offended
               if you change them.

RAY   Oh they're fine . . . fine. They'll do for now.

PETER   And the hot water tank is a bit
               temperamental. It might wake you up in the
               morning making a huge racket. But it rather
               depends in its mood. Sometimes it's quiet as
               a lamb. It's a wonderful house.

RAY   Yes it is.

PETER   Yes. We had . . . many happy years here.
               There.

               (PETER *sits in the deck chair and picks up
               the radio. Sound of static, then he tunes in a
               music station: 1930s orchestral. He settles
               back and listens, conducting the music with
               a waving arm.* SUSAN *returns to the window
               – coughs.* RAY *turns, she motions him back.*)

SUSAN   Where does he think he is – The last night of
               the Bloody Proms?

RAY   How did you get on?

SUSAN   Waste of time. Bloody woman.

RAY   I thought you liked her. You said she was a
               very decent person to do business with.

SUSAN   Well that was before she dumped her
                 husband on us.

RAY   So he was included in the contract?

SUSAN   She said that as far as she was concerned
                 he was no longer her responsibility. After
                 looking after him for nearly forty years she
                 said that it was time for somebody else to
                 take their turn – unless he chooses to take
                 responsibility for himself – which she thinks
                 is unlikely.

RAY   Great.

SUSAN   Well I'm not going to have it.

RAY   What are you going to do?

SUSAN   Kick him out.

RAY   You can't!

SUSAN   I'm not going to attack him – I'm just going
                 to appeal to his sense of decency.

                 (*She opens the door and goes out to confront
                 him.* RAY *follows at a short distance.* PETER
                 *has now opened the wine, which he is
                 drinking from the cup of the thermos.*)

PETER   Oh hello. Would you like a glass of wine?
                 You'll have to supply the glass I'm afraid.

SUSAN   You have to leave. Now.

PETER   Ah.

SUSAN   I'm sorry. I've spoken to your wife and she's
                 explained the circumstances but we can't
                 have you out here any longer.

PETER   You spoke to my wife?

SUSAN   Yes.

PETER   Was she with the nudist psychiatrist or the lorry driver? Simon, or Steven? I can't remember which is which now.

SUSAN   She didn't say.

PETER   You were lucky to catch her. I imagine she'll soon be on her way to the port to board a cruise ship for the Mediterranean – penning an ode as she drives along . . . Although I think she'll be hard pressed to find anything to rhyme with Mediterranean.

(PETER *thinks a bit.*)

SUSAN   Shall I call you a taxi?

PETER   That won't be necessary.

SUSAN   You'll leave on foot?

PETER   No. I'm not leaving.

SUSAN   But you must.

PETER   I have nowhere to go.

SUSAN   You have everywhere to go. Everywhere that's not here.

PETER   I have no intention of leaving.

SUSAN   You're going to squat?

PETER   No, I'm going to remain seated. I can't squat on these knees.

SUSAN   No. I mean legally squat.

PETER   I don't know. I hadn't thought of that but
               yes, I suppose I am.

SUSAN   So we're going to have to go through the
               rigmarole of getting you removed legally?

PETER   I suppose so. If you must.

SUSAN   All right. If you want it that way.

PETER   I wonder why they call it squatting. Do
               you suppose it's because the places these
               people get into don't have furniture so
               they're forced to squat both literally and
               metaphorically?

SUSAN   Forty years?

PETER   What?

SUSAN   How did your wife manage forty years?

               (*She storms off, pausing at the French
               windows.*)

PETER   Well I managed forty years with her too
               remember. This, I should add, is a woman
               who intends to bathe naked in Bexhill-on-
               Sea, who intends to paint and write poetry
               and cavort around the Mediterranean on a
               cruise ship with an unqualified psychiatrist
               who I'm convinced is only after her money.
               She'll be back. Mark my words.

SUSAN   Well the sooner the better.

PETER   I'll drink to that. (*Raises glass.*) Are you
               sure you won't take a drink?

SUSAN   I don't want a drink with you. We brought a
          bottle of champagne to celebrate moving in
          to our new home.

PETER   Well, thank you but champagne gives me
          indigestion.

SUSAN   I wasn't offering you a glass, you . . .

          (*She draws in a deep breath and exits.* RAY
          winces an apology towards PETER. *The
          French doors are slammed.* RAY *remains
          outside on the patio – hands in pockets.*
          PETER *takes another drink and sinks back
          into his deck chair.* RAY *wanders out.*)

RAY   You're seriously staying then?

PETER   Yes. I'm sorry. But yes I am.

RAY   For how long?

PETER   I don't know.

RAY   This is very difficult for us, you know.

PETER   I'm sorry. I understand.

RAY   Do you? What if . . . ?

          (*Turns to look inside the house. Furtive, he
          turns back.*)

RAY   What if I paid for you to stay in a hotel?
          For a week. Full board. Just until you found
          somewhere else.

PETER   The money is not the issue. This is my
          home. I can't . . . I can't conceive of being
          somewhere else. You can understand that?

(RAY *nods*.)

RAY   I don't understand how it happened.

PETER   Neither do I. I mean I thought we had a good
             marriage. We talked . . . We liked the same
             things – cricket – well obviously she didn't
             like cricket, she liked me liking cricket,
             which I think amounts to the same thing in
             marriage doesn't it?

RAY   Of course.

PETER   And books. She liked books. And . . . many
             other things I'm sure. But we both took
             an interest in the others' interests. From a
             distance – from a distance. She was always
             reading and telling me about it and I was
             very good at pretending an interest – as
             was she. And she did like going away. Long
             weekends – to places of historic interest. On
             coaches. Which she very much enjoyed. I
             admit she tended to go on her own because
             I've always been a bit of a home bird and
             she has always loved to travel. But I never
             stood in her way – ever. Yes, we had an
             awful lot in common.

RAY   Did you have children?

PETER   No. On the issue of children we were both
             of a very similar mind in that we didn't
             want them cluttering up our lives. I was
             very resolute on that one and Ruth, she . . .
             When we lost the first, and then the second,
             well she . . . She came round to my way of
             thinking.

             (RAY *nods*.)

PETER   It's important to be of the same mind. It
             keeps a marriage alive.

(RAY *nods. Looks back towards the house.*)

RAY   Well. I suppose I'd better get back in.

PETER   Yes, it wouldn't do to be seen fraternising
             with the enemy.

RAY   No.

PETER   Good night.

(RAY *saunters off. Lights fade.*)

Scene Four

Night. Lights fade up on the garden lit only by the moon and
PETER's *Calor gas light which emits a small globe of yellow
light. He's in his deck chair, waxed coat on, cricket cap on,
tarpaulin covering him. He's listening to the music on the
radio.*

*We see the flash of blue lights sweeping the stage and hear
the sound of a car drawing up. A door slams. Police r/t
static. A moment of interest from* PETER, *indicated by a quick
raising of his head.*

A uniformed POLICEMAN *appears at the French window with*
SUSAN *and* RAY. *The doors are shut. We can see them talking
but we can't hear what they're saying.*

The POLICEMAN *nods and comes out, closing the door behind
him. He approaches the deck chair and stands formally
beside it.*

POLICEMAN   Good evening, sir.

PETER   Evening officer.

POLICEMAN   Mild night, isn't it?

PETER   Extremely.

POLICEMAN   You're no doubt aware of why I'm here.

PETER   Yes. As you're also no doubt aware of why I
                 am here. So perhaps we could save ourselves
                 an unnecessary conversation and wish each
                 other good night.

POLICEMAN   You know you're trespassing?

PETER   No. I'm not.

POLICEMAN   It's not your property, sir, so I would suggest
                 that you are in fact trespassing.

PETER   But it was my property when I entered it.
                 'Trespass', as you may be aware, is derived
                 from the Latin trans, meaning across, and
                 passus, the act of going from place to place.
                 Unless I leave and return I don't think I can
                 be accused of trespassing.

POLICEMAN   I'm afraid I didn't have the benefit of a
                 private education, sir, so I didn't study
                 Latin.

PETER   You should take it up. It's extremely useful
                 in circumstances such as these.

POLICEMAN   I have very little time for new hobbies.

PETER   I'm sure you could find an evening class in
                 it somewhere.

POLICEMAN   I'm afraid my shifts make regular evening
                 classes impossible.

PETER   Even if you told your Chief Constable you
                 were going to study Latin?

POLICEMAN	I don't think he'd consider that sufficient grounds for regular shifts.
PETER	That's very short-sighted of him. I'm sure it would halve the crime rate virtually overnight.
POLICEMAN	So you're not going to leave?
PETER	No.
POLICEMAN	. . . You seem a decent man, sir, if you don't mind me saying.
PETER	I don't mind you saying that at all.
POLICEMAN	A sensitive man?
PETER	I'd like to think so.
POLICEMAN	Then you'll have put yourself in the place of the new occupants and imagined how they must be feeling.
PETER	I have. And I have concluded that they are probably not hugely pleased with the idea of me living in their garden.
POLICEMAN	And that doesn't concern you?
PETER	It concerns me – but not to the extent I intend to leave.

(*New music on radio – A tango. The* POLICEMAN'S *attention is caught by it. A pause.* PETER *picks up on the interest.*)

PETER	You're interested in music?

POLICEMAN   The tango, sir. I mentioned I had little time
             for new hobbies – but my wife and I are
             keen ballroom dancers.

PETER   And you specialize in the Tango?

POLICEMAN   My wife favours the Mambo and the Swing
             Boogie – I'm more of a Tango man, myself.

PETER   My wife was always keen to learn to dance.

POLICEMAN   She didn't take it up?

PETER   No. She has weak ankles.

             (*The* POLICEMAN *listens closer.*)

POLICEMAN   Carlos Gardel. Have you ever eard of him?

PETER   No. I can't say I have.

POLICEMAN   Great hero of mine. Dancer in the 1920s. If
             you get an opportunity to see him on film I
             recommend taking it up.

PETER   I shall.

             (*The* POLICEMAN *does a few tango steps.*)

PETER   That's most impressive. Graceful.

POLICEMAN   You're kind to say so, sir. I've often been
             praised for my fleetfootedness. Useful both
             on the dance floor and in pursuing young
             scrotes who are after having it away on foot.

PETER   You missed your true vocation.

             (*The* POLICEMAN *dances some more, leading
             an imaginary partner round the garden.*)

PETER   Bravo!

                         (*The* POLICEMAN *continues to dance. He*
                         pauses, extends a hand in invitation. Coyly,
                         PETER *rises, and takes up the offer. Now, in*
                         each other's arms, they process round the
                         stage. Slow light up on RAY *and* SUSAN *at*
                         the window – RAY *with a smile on his face,*
                         SUSAN *watching the scene with growing*
                         incredulity. She slides open the door and
                         comes out, standing, arms crossed, looking
                         towards the dancers with fury.)

PETER   Oh. Good evening. Have you come to join
                         us?

                         (*She ignores him.*)

SUSAN   (*to* POLICEMAN) What are you doing?

POLICEMAN   I'm demonstrating the basic steps of the
                         Tango ma'am.

SUSAN   Forgive me, officer. But did the message get
                         muddled on its way to you?

POLICEMAN   Message?

SUSAN   Yes. When I called the station I asked
                         for someone to come round and evict
                         a trespasser from the premises – not to
                         conduct an impromptu dancing display.

                         (PETER *and the* POLICEMAN *come to a stop and*
                         release their clench.)

POLICEMAN   Yes. I'm sorry. But I explained to the
                         gentleman the circumstances and he
                         explained to me that he is not, in fact,
                         trespassing.

PETER   Indeed not. I . . .

SUSAN   Be quiet. (*To* POLICEMAN.) How can he not be
                trespassing?

POLICEMAN   He has not entered the property. Therefore
                an act of trespass has not occurred. Unless
                he leaves and then attempts to re-enter, he is
                allowed to remain here unless and until you
                secure a court possession order.

SUSAN   So you can do nothing?

POLICEMAN   I'm afraid not.

SUSAN   Then good night.

POLICEMAN   Good night ma'am.

PETER   Good night.

POLICEMAN   Sir.

                (*He exits.* SUSAN *looks at him.*)

SUSAN   You don't pull the wool over my eyes, Mr
                Rattenbury.

PETER   I'm attempting to pull no wool over
                anybody's eyes.

SUSAN   My husband might have bought this helpless
                victim act but I can see right through you.

PETER   I'm sorry you feel that way.

SUSAN   Then leave us in peace to enjoy our new
                house – and new life. Go and make a fresh
                start yourself.

                (*No response.*)

SUSAN   Then I hope it rains.

                         (She storms off. Slamming the door. PETER *looks up at the moon. A clap of thunder. Slow fade out on lights and music.)*

ACT TWO

Scene One

The dining room – Day.

Susan is taking down the long curtains. Ray is rummaging through a box. There are a number of removal boxes in the room – some open, some taped shut. Sound of heavy rain.

SUSAN	They are horrible aren't they?
	(*She drops the heavy curtains on the floor.*)
RAY	Yes. Dreadful.
SUSAN	That's other peoples' taste for you.
RAY	Bad taste is bad taste.
SUSAN	No. Bad taste is other peoples' taste.
RAY	And good taste is our taste?
SUSAN	(*smiles*) Yes. Exactly.
RAY	Which of course everybody believes.
SUSAN	Yes. But everybody else is in the wrong.
RAY	Except us.
SUSAN	Yes. Exactly. Why hasn't that solicitor rung back?
RAY	I'm sure he will.
SUSAN	How long do think it'll take to get the possession order thing?

RAY	I don't know. But if it goes on raining he might just wander off of his own accord.
SUSAN	No chance.
	(*She looks at the curtains.* RAY *is now taking out a number of paperback books from the box.*)
SUSAN	What are you doing?
RAY	I'm emptying the box.
SUSAN	Of books?
RAY	Yes. Books. (*Reads side of box.*) 'Content of box: Books'. See . . . ?
	(*Holds up the books.*)
SUSAN	The books go in the lounge.
RAY	Yes. I'm taking them through into the lounge when I've got them all out.
SUSAN	One by one?
RAY	(*slight annoyance*) Or two by two, or three or four. I don't know. I haven't decided on the exact quantities yet. When I do I'll let you know.
SUSAN	There's no need to be facetious.
RAY	Well why don't you let me get on with unpacking and you can get on with taking down the curtains. I won't tell you how to do that and, in return, why don't you try and stop telling me how to unpack a box.
SUSAN	Suit yourself.

(*A pause.* RAY *takes out more books. Then pauses again.* SUSAN *folds the curtains.*)

RAY   (*something begins to dawn*) What's that supposed to mean?

SUSAN   'Suit yourself'?

RAY   Yes.

SUSAN   It means exactly that: Suit yourself in the way you're choosing to waste time emptying that box.

RAY   How exactly am I wasting time?

SUSAN   If you don't know then I'm not going to waste my time telling you.

               (RAY *continues. Thinks a bit. Pauses.*)

RAY   Well go on.

               (SUSAN, *having started unclipping the other curtains, pauses.*)

SUSAN   So how are you going to get those books into the lounge?

RAY   (*irony*) Let's see. Well. I thought I'd carry them. Okay, Susan?

SUSAN   Two or three at a time.

RAY   Yes.

SUSAN   What does it say on the box, Ray?

RAY   It says: "Contents: Books. Room: lounge."

SUSAN   Correct.

RAY   Which is where I'm taking them. Okay?

SUSAN   Would it not therefore be simpler to take
             the box into the lounge and unpack it there?
             Thus avoiding the need for ten or fifteen
             unnecessary journeys?

             (*This dawns on* RAY *as an unavoidable
             truth.*)

RAY   (*uncertain*) No.

SUSAN   And why not?

RAY   Because the box is too heavy to move.

SUSAN   Then empty it a bit.

             (*She turns to the curtains.* RAY *mimes a face
             at her back.*)

RAY   Good idea.

             (*He goes on emptying the box, stacking the
             books on the floor. A crack of thunder.* RAY
             *looks up. He looks back down at the box and
             tries to move it. Still too heavy. He takes
             out more books. They conduct the following
             backs to each other.*)

RAY   I don't see why you need all these books
             anyway. You don't read them.

SUSAN   That's why I've got them. Because I'm going
             to read them.

RAY   You've never read a book in your life.

SUSAN   I have too.

RAY   What was it called?

SUSAN	There have been so many.
RAY	Susan, we have been living together for ten years and never once in all that time have I seen you reading a book. A magazine, yes. A book, no.
SUSAN	I read at night. In bed.
RAY	We share the same bed. I think I'd have noticed if you were reading.
SUSAN	Would you? Your eyes shut as soon as your head hits the pillow.
RAY	So do yours.
SUSAN	They don't. They stay open and I read. There is always a book beside my bed. And there has been in the ten years we've been together.
RAY	Yes. And it's always been the same one. By Joanna Trollope: *A Village Affair*. Your sister bought it for you for Christmas 1998 and it still has the bookmark at page three.
SUSAN	I use it to keep my book mark flat.
RAY	Because you whiz through the other books so fast it needs straightening out?
SUSAN	Yes.
RAY	All right. Tell me the last one you read cover to cover without me noticing you doing it.
SUSAN	*Pride and Prejudice*.
RAY	Was it good?

SUSAN   It was excellent. A real page-turner.

RAY   And what was it about?

                 (*He picks up a book:* Pride and Prejudice
                 and begins examining it.)

SUSAN   Oh, you know. Pretty much what you'd
                 expect from the title.

RAY   Pride?

SUSAN   Yes. Proud people and . . . deeply prejudiced
                 people.

RAY   Really? What about the story?

SUSAN   Mm?

RAY   The story. What was it about?

SUSAN   Well. . . It was set in the 1950s and it was
                 about people from the Caribbean coming in
                 to be bus drivers and working in the NHS.
                 And people being prejudiced against them.

RAY   And the proud?

SUSAN   That was them. They were proud to be
                 working.

RAY   (*reads from cover*) It wasn't a "sensitive
                 insight into manners, morality and marriage
                 in the early 19th century"?

SUSAN   No. It was about a bus driver called Winston.

RAY   Susan?

                 (*She turns.* RAY *holds up the cover.*)

SUSAN   What's that?

RAY   *Pride and Prejudice.* By Jane Austen.

SUSAN   What a nerve.

RAY   What?

SUSAN   She must have stolen the title.

             (RAY *looks at the book.*)

RAY   In 1813.

SUSAN   Yes. Some writers will stop at nothing.

             (RAY *shakes his head – pushes box. It will
             now move. He slides it across the floor
             towards the door.* SUSAN *sees the books on
             the floor.*)

SUSAN   I do hope you're not going to leave those
             books on the floor.

             (*A pause.* RAY *straightens himself. Stretches
             out his back – and walks out.*)

SUSAN   Where are you going?

RAY   Out!

             (*Another clap of thunder. When* RAY *has
             gone,* SUSAN *puts the kettle on. Then goes to
             the window. Now the garden is lit and we see*
             PETER *in his deckchair under the umbrella,
             dressed against the rain. His radio is on.
             Sound of commentary: Rain stopped play.*)

SUSAN   (*calls*) Comfortable?

PETER   Very. Thank you.

SUSAN	You're not cold and wet?
PETER	On the contrary, very cosy thanks.
SUSAN	I'm making a cup of tea.
PETER	(*with interest*) Are you?
SUSAN	Yes. Imagine what that must be like – just to be able to switch on a kettle and make a lovely hot drink for yourself.

(*She slams the window. Fade out.*)

Scene Two

The dining room/garden. An hour later. The dining room is empty. The rain continues. In the garden PETER *is still under the umbrella.*

RAY	(*off*) Susan!

(RAY *enters the dining room. Looks at table. Picks up note. Reads.*)

RAY	'Gone shopping. Calling in to solicitor. I might pop into the library on way back. (RAY *shakes his head.*) Back about one. Don't worry about lunch. I'll bring something.'

(RAY *goes to window. Looks out. Looks up at rain. A pause. He opens the door.*)

RAY	(*calls*) Good morning.
PETER	(*turns his head round*) Oh. Good morning.
RAY	Sleep well?
PETER	Like a baby.

RAY	You weren't cold?
PETER	Not at all.
RAY	Wet?
PETER	No. The umbrella's working nicely. Rain stopped play at The Oval I'm afraid.
RAY	And what about food? Have you had breakfast?
PETER	Yes. My wife left me some sandwiches. Cheese and tomato. Filled the gap nicely. And I've been raiding the vegetable patch for salad I'm afraid.

(RAY *looks guiltily behind him.*)

RAY	Look. Do you want a cup of tea?
PETER	Is that wise?
RAY	Susan's out.
PETER	Ah. Well I wouldn't want to get you into trouble.
RAY	Just between us, Okay?
PETER	Understood.

(PETER *stands and dashes in through rain.*)

PETER	Thank you. Given the circumstances you're very kind.
RAY	You know where the toilet is?
PETER	Do you mind?

RAY   No. Go on.

               (PETER *exits.* RAY *puts on the kettle. Opens*
               cupboards. Gets out cup. Another clap of
               thunder. RAY *goes to the window. Looks out.*
               PETER *returns.*)

PETER   That's better. The veneer of civilisation is
               very thin isn't it?

RAY   I suppose so.

PETER   Shelter. Running water. A flushing toilet.
               Food. That's all. Everything else is frills.

RAY   And cricket?

PETER   Ah . . . Another essential.

               (RAY *pours.*)

RAY   Sugar?

PETER   No. Just milk. Thank you.

               (RAY *pours milk. Hands over the cup.*)

PETER   Thank you.

RAY   I should tell you that my wife is seeing the
               solicitor now.

PETER   Of course. In your shoes I'd do the same.

               (PETER *sips his tea. They do not meet each*
               others' eye.)

RAY   I still don't understand how it came to this.

PETER   Neither do I. I wish I did.

RAY   You had no idea?

PETER   None at all. I thought we were all
             right together. I worked hard. We were
             comfortably off. Ruth had her own work too
             – she worked for a small accountancy office
             doing bits and pieces – tax returns that kind
             of thing.

RAY   And you?

PETER   Light engineering. I managed a small
             company. Nothing grandiose. And suddenly
             forty years passed. In the blink of an
             eye. And I suppose – I suppose as she
             contemplated her mortality she decided
             she had missed out on life. On some great
             passion. I don't know. It's all a great shock.
             I think . . . I think women believe in passion
             far more than men. For women it's mental,
             which is much more potent. But I'm sure I
             don't need to tell you that.

RAY   Do you feel you missed out on something?

PETER   Of course. It's inevitable. But marriage is
             about weighing what you have against what
             you're missing. If the scales come down
             on the side of what you have then you stay
             married. If not, then you . . . go to Bexhill-
             on-Sea with a man called Steven.

RAY   But what if you don't know what you're
             missing. And you get tempted to try?

PETER   I can't answer that.

RAY   You've never . . . ?

PETER   No.

RAY	. . . Sometimes I think I don't know her at all.

PETER	Susan?

RAY	Sometimes I think she doesn't want me to know her. It's like she puts up this barrier and she's behind it – and if it was just her on the other side then I wouldn't mind, but there's other people too. Her friends. Her mother. I feel . . . on the other side of it.

(PETER *nods*.)

RAY	We're trying for children.

PETER	Oh Good.

RAY	Except we've been trying for five years. I don't know when it counts as . . . You know, just having sex again rather than 'trying for children'. I mean you don't normally tell everyone you know about your sex life, do you? But when you're trying for a baby it seems like it's all right. 'What are you doing tonight?' 'Oh, we're trying for a baby . . . ' It's not secret any more.

(PETER *nods*. RAY *smiles*.)

RAY	Listen to me. Pouring my heart out to a squatter.

PETER	The *Daily Mail* would have a field day.

(*Sound of key in lock.*)

RAY	Susan!

(PETER *drains his cup*.)

SUSAN	(*off*) Where are you?
PETER	Thank you.
RAY	(*calls*) In here. (*To* PETER.) Listen. What we just talked about . . .
PETER	Lips are sealed. I promise.
	(*He dashes out, handing the cup to* RAY, *who closes the door. Dashes to the sink and rinses the cup.* SUSAN *enters, coat on.*)
SUSAN	You're washing up?
RAY	Absolutely, my precious.
SUSAN	(*suspicious*) What have you done?
RAY	(*innocent*) What?
SUSAN	You never wash up.
	(*She looks round the room.*)
SUSAN	What have you broken?
RAY	I . . . I've not broken anything. I just wanted to apologize for storming out. That's all.
SUSAN	Well apology accepted. And if you are going to wash up then please use washing up liquid, otherwise I'll have to do it all again and we'll both have wasted our time, won't we?
	(*She exits.* RAY *pulls a frustrated face.*)
SUSAN	(*off*) I saw Mr Chivers.
RAY	Yes?

SUSAN	(*off*) He said we might be able to get something called an interim possession order. We'll have to go to court, though.
RAY	Sounds expensive.

(SUSAN *re-enters without her coat on.*)

SUSAN	Yes. Well it's worth it. I don't want him here any longer than necessary.

(*She goes to the window and peers out.*)

SUSAN	What has he been doing?
RAY	Listening to the radio. Sheltering from the rain.
SUSAN	Well it's almost stopped now. Unfortunately.
RAY	You could try and put yourself in his shoes, you know.

(SUSAN *turns to face him.*)

SUSAN	What?
RAY	He hasn't got anywhere to go.
SUSAN	Don't be ridiculous! This house cost us enough for him to live in a five star hotel for at least ten years. Don't get taken in by him. I told you. He's a type and he's just trying to make us feel guilty. He'll be asking for a cup of tea before you know it.

(RAY *can't help but allow his eyes to the cup on the draining board.* SUSAN *looks at it. Then across to the cup on the table. She knows.*)

SUSAN   I don't believe it. I do not believe it!

RAY   Look . . .

SUSAN   Pathetic. You are pathetic!

RAY   He's an old man.

SUSAN   He is in his early sixties. Nowadays that's
             considered barely middle-aged.

RAY   Okay. Well he's been outside all night – and
             he's cold.

SUSAN   And whose fault is that!

RAY   Look . . .

SUSAN   Look? At what? Look in the mirror – look
             at someone who's got 'mug' written all over
             her forehead?

RAY   You're upset. I can understand that. The
             move was stressful enough, and now this . . .

SUSAN   Yes. The move was stressful enough. But I
             coped. And this was extra stress, but I coped.
             And I coped because I thought we were in
             it together. But we're not, are we? As usual
             it's Ray and his bleeding heart against hard-
             hearted Susan.

             (*Pause.*)

SUSAN   (*with venom*) God knows what it would be
             like if we ever did manage to have children.
             God knows! It'd be, 'daddy lets us do this,
             why are you being so horrible, mummy?'
             Yes? Would I have to be the bad one all the
             time just to teach them how hard the world
             is?

RAY   The world is as hard as you make it, Susan.

SUSAN   One of us has to be a realist. There isn't
           room for two idealists in a marriage.

           (SUSAN *shakes her head.* RAY *sighs and goes
           to the door. He opens it.*)

SUSAN   What are you doing?

RAY   (*angry*) Getting some fresh air.

SUSAN   If you go out there you can stay out there.

RAY   What?

SUSAN   If that's where you'd rather be – with a
           lonely old man listening to the cricket in his
           garden.

RAY   If I ever get old, Susan, I'd be more than
           happy sitting on a deck chair in the garden
           listening to the cricket.

SUSAN   But I assume that would be in your own
           garden on your own deck chair?

RAY   Well . . .

SUSAN   Not much to look forward to is it?

RAY   I don't know. I think I'd be very happy if I
           reached that level of contentment.

SUSAN   Like him?

RAY   Yes.

SUSAN   The mad are always happy, Ray, because
           they don't know they're mad. It's the people
           around them who suffer. He drove his wife

	mad for forty years. How much contentment and peace did she have?
RAY	So we keep hearing. So why put up with it?
SUSAN	Because that's what women do.
	(*The phone rings.* SUSAN *looks at it.* RAY *looks at it. Neither go for it.*)
RAY	It'll be your mother.
SUSAN	No it won't. I've just left her.
RAY	You said you went to town.
SUSAN	And I saw mum, and we had a coffee and we talked.
RAY	You didn't mention it.
SUSAN	You didn't ask.
RAY	You mentioned the solicitor, the library, but not your mother.
SUSAN	There was nothing sinister about it.
RAY	If it was your mother, then I beg to differ.
SUSAN	That was cheap.
RAY	So – what about?
SUSAN	What?
RAY	What did you talk about?
SUSAN	Oh, for God's sake.

(She goes to the phone and she picks it up.)

SUSAN   Hello? . . . Oh, Mrs Rattenbury, yes we were
          just talking about you *(Turns to* RAY.) . . .
          Yes . . . Yes, I'm afraid he is still here.

          *(She takes the cordless phone to the window
          and looks out.)*

SUSAN   . . . Sitting on his deckchair, under his
          umbrella, on OUR lawn, listening to the
          radio . . . Really? . . . No, I'd rather you
          didn't . . . Well if you want to meet up with
          him I suggest you find a cafe or a restaurant
          and do it there, I'd be more than happy
          to pass on a message to him . . . No, I'm
          sorry, I have no intention of letting you
          in the house. One member of your family
          in permanent residence is enough . . . No.
          Goodbye.

          (She puts down the phone.)

SUSAN   Bloody nerve.

RAY   What?

SUSAN   She says she wants to come and see him.
          Well, you heard the conversation.

RAY   Why?

SUSAN   I don't know.

RAY   Well maybe if she came she could talk him
          into leaving.

SUSAN   Or maybe she'd bring another deck chair and
          move in with him. They probably planned it
          from the beginning.

RAY	Unlikely, I'd say.
SUSAN	Well, yes, you would consider it unlikely, but that's just another example of you seeing the best in people – and being let down.
RAY	Or proved right.

(RAY *is at the door.*)

RAY	Surely worth a try isn't it?
SUSAN	Is it?
RAY	Oh, come on, Susan. Do you really want to spend a couple of grand and who knows how much time and aggro going to court? Call her. I'm sure he's looking for an excuse to leave. He just doesn't want to look foolish.
SUSAN	Too late.
RAY	Call her back.
SUSAN	You call her. Why do I have to do everything?

(*She hands him the phone.*)

SUSAN	She comes in through the side gate – not through the house. We do not invite her across the threshold. She can have no more than fifteen minutes and then she leaves.

(RAY *nods.*)

SUSAN	(*softer*) I'd like to be proved wrong, Ray. About people being bad, and letting you down all the time. But I spend all my life being proved right.

RAY   That doesn't say a lot about me, does it?

SUSAN   You don't count.

RAY   Why?

SUSAN   Because you're my husband and you have to
            be on my side.

RAY   So, despite that – despite the fact that I
            chose you and I'm always on your side –
            and I have never let you down – well, not in
            any big way – you still prefer to believe the
            worst in people.

            (*She looks away, then leaves the room.*)

RAY   What did she do to you?

            (RAY *looks after her. He dials.*)

RAY   Mrs Rattenbury? . . . Hello, yes, it's Ray
            Haslam . . . Yes, you just spoke to my wife
            . . . Look, we've just had a talk and we think
            it might be an idea if you did come to see
            your husband . . . Yes . . .

            (*Fade out.*)

ACT THREE

Scene One

The garden – Day.

The sun is out. PETER *is in his deck chair listening to the third day of the cricket. He is in a short-sleeved shirt and light trousers. He looks better established in the garden – everything around him is neatly squared away. He is unshaven. His habitual neatness is breaking down.*

SUSAN *is at the window in a summer dress – she's watching him. She opens the door and comes out. She looks up at the sun.*

PETER   (*cranes his neck round, speaks brightly*)
                 Good morning.

                 (*She doesn't answer.*)

PETER   Would you like a deck chair? There's another
                 in the shed?

SUSAN   No. Thank you.

                 (*She comes a few steps further out.*)

PETER   Settling in?

SUSAN   Inside the house. Yes. Less so outside.

                 (PETER *nods.*)

PETER   And how is your husband?

SUSAN   His back's bad, otherwise fine.

PETER   Good. I like Ray. We get on like a house on
                 fire.

SUSAN   You've got a lot in common.

PETER   (*pleased*) Yes. We have, haven't we?

                 (*A pause.*)

SUSAN   Your wife is coming.

PETER   My wife?

SUSAN   She's coming at mid-day today. She wants to
                 see you.

PETER   Will she be delivered by the nudist therapist
                 or the lorry driver?

SUSAN   I don't know how she's getting here and I
                 don't care. Ray told her she can have fifteen
                 minutes and then she must go. Hopefully
                 taking you with her.

PETER   I made it very clear to her that under no
                 circumstances would I board a cruise ship so
                 if she's bought tickets she'll have wasted her
                 money.

SUSAN   She didn't mention anything about a cruise.

PETER   Good.

SUSAN   . . . But if somebody bought me tickets to go
                 on a cruise – Ray, for example – I think I'd
                 be very pleased.

PETER   Awful things, cruise ships. A haven for
                 disease: cholera, norovirus. You hear about
                 it all the time – people wading ankle deep in
                 faecal matter, projectile vomiting . . . Awful.

SUSAN   I'm sure most cruise ships manage to sail
                 without any problem at all.

PETER   So my wife tried to convince me.

SUSAN   But you didn't listen?

PETER   No. I listened and then I took issue with her.
            And she came round to my point of view.

SUSAN   How sad.

PETER   Not sad at all. My wife is the least sad
            person I know.

SUSAN   She sounds like a saint to me.

PETER   Well to some extent . . . Yes, she was always
            a very accommodating person.

SUSAN   Unlike you?

PETER   Oh, I'm very accommodating.

SUSAN   To her?

PETER   Yes. Of course.

SUSAN   It doesn't sound like it to me.

PETER   You barely know me so I fail to see how you
            can make a judgement.

SUSAN   Would it have hurt to go on a cruise ship with
            her? Just once? Because it sounds to me that
            it's something she really wanted to do – and
            I suppose she wanted to do it with you – God
            knows why – but you talked her out of it.

PETER   I didn't talk her out of it. I merely pointed
            out . . .

SUSAN   You made it sound so terrible she gave up . . .
            Yes?

PETER	Well, I expect I could have . . . I mean.
SUSAN	In other things, then? What did you ever do for her?
PETER	Many things. Too numerous to mention.
SUSAN	Tell me one.
PETER	Well I . . . I bought her flowers. Every Friday. I bought them from the same stall on the station every week and she loved it.
SUSAN	Habit. Nothing felt. Just habit.
PETER	She loved the flowers. At least she said she did.
SUSAN	All right. Apart from the flowers . . . ?
PETER	Young lady. Nice as it is to chat to you, I am trying to listen to the cricket – which is reaching quite a crucial stage.
SUSAN	Ah . . .
PETER	I'm sorry?
SUSAN	Nothing.
PETER	You said "ah".
SUSAN	That's right.
PETER	In such a way as to convey you'd made another rash judgement about me.
SUSAN	Perhaps.
PETER	Would you care to share it?

SUSAN   I'd hate to interrupt your cricket.

PETER   Please go on. I'm intrigued.

SUSAN   Cricket. You use it as an excuse.

PETER   Hardly.

SUSAN   Yes. You do. When things become
             uncomfortable you use it to hide.

PETER   Ridiculous.

SUSAN   Not ridiculous at all. Please, go on listening.

             (*A sudden pain.* SUSAN *clutches her
             stomach.*)

PETER   Are you all right?

SUSAN   Yes.

PETER   Are you sure?

             (*He stands.* SUSAN *is still in discomfort.*)

PETER   Here. Sit down. Please.

             (SUSAN *sits.*)

PETER   Can I get you some water or something?

             (*He heads for the house.*)

SUSAN   You are not going into the house!

             (*He stops, half way.*)

PETER   Is Ray in? Shall I call him?

SUSAN	No. He's in town.

(She breathes deeply. She regains her composure.)

SUSAN	I'm all right.
PETER	Sure?
SUSAN	Yes. Please don't fuss.

(PETER hovers over her.)

PETER	And how long have you been pregnant?

(She looks at him.)

SUSAN	How do you know?
PETER	I knew the first time I saw you. You have the same kind of glow that Ruth did.
SUSAN	Six weeks.
PETER	And Ray is not aware of this?
SUSAN	No. Ray is not aware of this.

(PETER nods.)

SUSAN	You see?
PETER	See what?
SUSAN	You're not stupid, or unseeing. You do notice things.
PETER	Yes.

SUSAN	Which makes what you did to your wife much worse. You could see the misery you inflicted on her but you chose to go on doing it.

PETER	I think misery is a bit harsh.

SUSAN	All right. You were selfish. And she suffered for it.

(PETER *turns away*.)

PETER	My wife is coming at mid-day, you said?

SUSAN	Yes.

PETER	Well I'd better tidy up a bit.

(SUSAN *stands. Breathes deeply.* RAY *comes to the window.* SUSAN *and* PETER *have their backs to him. He backs off and listens. They're not aware of him being there.*)

PETER	You're sure you're all right?

SUSAN	Yes.

PETER	So you'll tell Ray?

SUSAN	Perhaps.

PETER	You must.

SUSAN	If I choose to keep it.

PETER	You're surely not considering . . . I mean given the efforts you've made over the last five years.

SUSAN	What?

PETER   To have a child.

SUSAN   How the hell do you know that?

PETER   Well . . .

SUSAN   He told you?

PETER   Yes.

SUSAN   Anything else?

PETER   No.

SUSAN   How cosy.

PETER   He was very loyal to you.

SUSAN   No he wasn't. If he was loyal he would have
             kept his mouth shut. Well as you seem to be
             party to all of the details of our private life I
             might as well tell you that my mother says I
             shouldn't keep the baby.

PETER   How terrible.

SUSAN   She says Ray and I don't have a future. I
             could do better. A child needs to be born into
             a stable, loving family.

PETER   I'm sure Ray loves you.

SUSAN   But do I love him? Looking at you, am I
             looking at Ray in thirty odd years time?
             Because, believe me, I'd have gone to
             Bexhill-on-Sea much sooner.

             (*We see* RAY *dart back, out of sight, and exit.*
             SUSAN *heads back to the house.* PETER *looks
             at the radio. The commentary continues.
             Fade out.*)

Scene Two

The house. Half an hour later.

SUSAN is in the kitchen. The clock shows 11.45. She is sitting at the table, tea cup in front of her, staring into space.

The front door opens and slams. SUSAN pulls herself together. RAY comes in. He has a unbranded carrier bag with him. Both are cagey.

SUSAN	How did you get on?
RAY	Fine. You?
SUSAN	Fine.
RAY	What have you been up to?
	(*He puts down the bag onto the table.*)
SUSAN	Tidying around.
RAY	Chatting to the squatter?
SUSAN	God forbid.
	(RAY *goes to the window.*)
RAY	Did you tell him his wife was coming?
	(SUSAN *is uncomfortable.*)
SUSAN	Oh yes. I told him about that.
RAY	And how did he take it?
SUSAN	He said he hoped she wasn't going to try and force him to go on a cruise ship.

(RAY *turns*.)

RAY   Is that likely do you think?

SUSAN   Who knows.

             (*A pause*.)

SUSAN   What have you got there?

RAY   A surprise.

SUSAN   For me?

RAY   Yes.

SUSAN   How exciting.

             (RAY *smiles*.)

SUSAN   Can I open it now?

RAY   Not yet.

SUSAN   Spoilsport.

             (RAY *looks up at clock*.)

RAY   She'll be here soon.

SUSAN   Yes – and then perhaps we'll get our house
             back.

RAY   Why did she stay with him?

SUSAN   Who knows.

RAY   I was thinking about it in town. Why stay for
             so long if she was unhappy?

SUSAN	Habit I suppose. Perhaps he entertained her. Perhaps she felt sorry for him. Sympathy is a terrible trap sometimes. And she was one of the last generation of those ridiculous decent people.
RAY	What's wrong with decency?
SUSAN	Decency is . . . smiling bravely when you don't get what you want or deserve. It's the British curse.
RAY	Isn't it about being good to other people?
SUSAN	Yes. At the cost to yourself.
RAY	That's a very depressing view of life.
SUSAN	Not at all.

(*She looks at the bag.*)

SUSAN	Can I open it now?
RAY	No. Not yet.
SUSAN	When then?
RAY	In a minute.

(*Distant sound of car pulling up. Door opens.*)

SUSAN	I think that's her. Open the door.
RAY	Absolutely not. They deserve some privacy.
SUSAN	(*pointedly*) Do they?
RAY	Yes.

(*Distant sound of car pulling away. Lights down in house. Lights up on garden. Creak of metal gate.* RUTH *enters with a wide brimmed hat and a very colourful and short dress on.* PETER *stands.*)

PETER   Good grief!

(RUTH *smiles.*)

RUTH   Do you like it?

(*She twirls.*)

PETER   It's almost indecent. I can almost see your underwear.

RUTH   I'm not wearing any.

PETER   Good Grief!

RUTH   It's the modern fashion. The young parade their underwear – or lack of it – at every opportunity. Have you not noticed?

PETER   It might have escaped your notice, Ruth, but you're not young. And I don't make a habit of inspecting other peoples' underwear.

RUTH   Well you should. I told a boy on the bus his trousers were falling down and he assured me he was intentionally displaying his underpants.

PETER   Why?

RUTH   Ventilation, perhaps. And as for women's foundation garments. Well, I'm afraid a sturdy gusset has gone the way of good manners from shopkeepers.

(*A pause.*)

RUTH   So how are you?

            (PETER *nods.*)

PETER   Given the circumstances, remarkably well.

RUTH   You've lost weight.

PETER   Yes. I've run out of sandwiches.

RUTH   When did you last eat?

PETER   Oh, I had a couple of tomatoes and spring
            onions this morning from the vegetable
            patch.

RUTH   No cucumbers?

PETER   I'm afraid the cucumbers aren't doing very
            well this year.

RUTH   What about the radishes?

PETER   I don't have my antacids.

RUTH   Well you can't survive on salad alone.
            You're not Greek.

PETER   I'm planning to snare a pigeon or two and
            cook it on the barbecue.

RUTH   You've become feral virtually overnight.

PETER   Needs must.

RUTH   And how are you going to go about snaring a
            pigeon?

PETER   Well I've been laying crumbs round the deckchair. A rather fat bird has been eyeing them with interest from next door's chimney breast.

(RUTH *looks up*.)

PETER   No. Don't look. He doesn't know I've spotted him. When he lands, I'll pounce.

RUTH   (*dismissive*) I'd like to see that.

PETER   You're welcome to stay and watch.

RUTH   You haven't pounced for at least twenty years.

PETER   I'm still capable of pouncing, I assure you, especially from a sitting position.

RUTH   So less of a pounce, more of an inelegant fall from the deck chair?

PETER   The pigeon will not know the difference I assure you.

RUTH   Wouldn't it be easier to go out for pigeon?

PETER   I can hardly do that, can I? They'd lock the gate and I wouldn't have anywhere to live.

RUTH   So you're intent on going on with this ridiculous charade?

PETER   I'm making a stand.

RUTH   Against what?

PETER   I haven't decided yet.

Ruth	Well when you do, it's good practice to let whoever you're making a stand against know, otherwise you'll be wasting your time.
Peter	Perhaps I'm making a stand against you.
Ruth	Well you're not affecting me so it's a futile gesture.
Peter	You're here, aren't you? You came back.
Ruth	Yes.
Peter	So it isn't an entirely futile gesture is it?
	(*Pause.*)
Peter	Shall I fetch another deck chair out?
Ruth	We don't have time. I'm rationed to fifteen minutes.
Peter	So how did you get here?
Ruth	Peter, I'm not going to describe the entire journey to you. I came by train and taxi.
Peter	From Bexhill-on-Sea?
Ruth	Yes.
Peter	And the lory driver chose not to drive you.
Ruth	I didn't ask him to.
Peter	Why not? Didn't you want us to meet?
Ruth	No.
Peter	So why did you come?

RUTH	To see how you were getting on.
PETER	As you can see, I'm doing very well. So goodbye. Toddle back to the lorry driver.
	(RUTH *looks hard at him.*)
RUTH	You wanted me to come back, then?
PETER	You were the one who chose to return.
RUTH	But you said that you were making a stand against me – and having come back, your stand worked.
PETER	Did it?
RUTH	Which would imply that you wanted me to come back.
	(*They look at each other.*)
PETER	I suppose I did.
RUTH	Why?
PETER	Because you're my wife.
RUTH	And wives are supposed to stay at home and do what they're told?
PETER	When have you ever done what you were told – in fact when have I ever tried to tell you to do anything?
RUTH	So why do you want me back?
PETER	Because I . . .
RUTH	You are allowed to say it, you know. It might be a four letter word but I won't be offended.

(*They remain facing each other from a distance of some feet. Lights out. Lights up in house.* SUSAN *and* RAY *are at the window looking out.*)

SUSAN   What a ridiculous dress.

RAY   It is a bit short, isn't it? Handsome woman, though.

SUSAN   She's nearly twice your age.

RAY   So?

SUSAN   They seem to be getting on well together.

RAY   How can you tell?

SUSAN   They like each other. It's obvious.

             (*She turns to* RAY.)

SUSAN   Will we still look at each other like that in forty years' time?

RAY   (*laughs*) What? If we bump into one another on the street?

SUSAN   Don't say that!

RAY   Why?

SUSAN   You're frightening me.

RAY   It happens. People separate.

             (*A pause.*)

SUSAN   So can I open my surprise?

RAY   If you want.

SUSAN	Will I like it?
	(RAY *goes to the bag.* SUSAN *joins him.*)
SUSAN	You've got a very serious look on your face, Ray. Am I going to like this surprise?
RAY	I hope so.
	(*He picks up the bag and hands it to her. She looks inside. She looks at* RAY.)
SUSAN	I don't understand.
	(*Lights out. Lights up on garden.*)
PETER	I love you.
RUTH	You see. It wasn't that hard, was it?
PETER	I've told you that many times. Almost every day of our lives together. But there is a harder word to say.
RUTH	Is there?
PETER	I've been . . . thinking – a lot, since you left.
RUTH	That will be the fresh air and the sun. It always perks you up. You're always gloomy in the winter.
PETER	It has been brought to my attention that I might not have been . . . very considerate of you.
RUTH	I've always found you to be most considerate.
PETER	But on the matter of cruises . . .

RUTH   Yes?

PETER   Perhaps we could have gone on one together.

RUTH   Oh, I'm not sure I could have stood that.

PETER   Why not?

RUTH   Well if either of us suffered a moment's
            sea-sickness then you'd insist on being
            helicoptered off immediately.

PETER   In the past, perhaps. But not now.

RUTH   You've changed your mind about cruise
            ships?

PETER   Yes.

RUTH   Entirely?

PETER   Almost entirely. Oh. And I also apologize
            about the flowers.

RUTH   What flowers?

PETER   The ones I bought you every week – from
            the same stall by platform fourteen.

RUTH   But I loved the flowers.

PETER   But I could have bought you something else
            once in a while.

RUTH   What?

PETER   I don't know. A hat, for example.

RUTH   I don't wear hats.

PETER   Chocolates, then.

RUTH   But what would I have put in the vase on
            Friday night? What would we have had on
            the dinner table if you didn't bring flowers?

PETER   I'm talking about the principle of flowers,
            Ruth. The principle of doing the same thing,
            week in, week out, without ever questioning
            it.

RUTH   But you're an engineer, darling. If
            I'd wanted somebody imaginative I'd
            have married an architect. I liked your
            predictability.

PETER   Until now.

            (*Again they face each other with
            seriousness.*)

PETER   You said I was odd.

RUTH   Not exactly odd.

PETER   Yes you did. You said I should have worked
            out that the man in the brown coat was a
            removal man and therefore the house had
            been cleared and therefore you were leaving
            me to go to Bexhill-on-Sea where you
            intended to frolic naked in the waves.

RUTH   I didn't expect you to deduce all that. You're
            not Sherlock Holmes.

PETER   Well what was it you were looking out of the
            bedroom window to see?

RUTH   Just . . . something recognizably normal.

PETER   You can't have it both ways, Ruth. You can't
            accuse me in one breath of predictability
            and then, in the next, of being abnormal.

Abnormality, by its very nature is hugely unpredictable.

RUTH   Not necessarily.

PETER   Why not?

RUTH   . . . You see?

PETER   See what?

RUTH   I'm trying to discuss the state of our marriage and now we're discussing whether or not abnormality can be predictable.

PETER   It's important to be clear about the terms we use. Otherwise confusion ensues.

RUTH   It's important to talk.

PETER   But that's what we are doing. We're very good at talking. You're surely not suggesting we talk about our feelings for each other are you?

RUTH   Heavens no, I don't think I'd be able to cope with that after all these years.

PETER   Then help me understand why you'd rather be in Bexhill-on-Sea with another man rather than me.

RUTH   . . . There is no other man.

PETER   What?

RUTH   I went alone.

PETER   The lorry driver left you already! Well you can't say I didn't warn you.

RUTH   He never existed. There is no Steven.

PETER   No lorry driver! And no therapist?

RUTH   Oh, there was a therapist. I think . . . I think
            that's why I got myself in such a tangle. He
            made me see things in a different way.

PETER   They have laws against that kind of thing.
            We'll have him struck off.

RUTH   I don't want him struck off.

PETER   And Bexhill-on-Sea?

RUTH   I have a flat there. Rented. For six months.

PETER   And the sea? Have you frolicked naked?

RUTH   I dipped a toe in the water. But it was too
            cold to go in any further.

            (*Lights down. Lights up inside the house.*
            SUSAN *is looking inside the bag.*)

SUSAN   I don't understand.

RAY   No?

SUSAN   What's the matter with you, Ray? I've never
            seen you look so serious. It doesn't suit you.

            (*She reaches in and takes out a Babygrow.
            She holds it up. Lights out. Lights up on
            garden. The commentary continues on the
            radio.* PETER *and* RUTH *are looking at each
            other – holding each other's hand.*)

PETER   And how do you find Bexhill-on-Sea?

| RUTH | Very agreeable. Although I can't profess to know it very well yet. |

| PETER | And does the flat have a sea view? |

| RUTH | Yes. |

| PETER | Access to a garden? |

| RUTH | Yes. |

| PETER | There is, of course, a cricket ground in the vicinity. How far away? |

| RUTH | 2.7 miles. |

| PETER | You checked? |

| RUTH | Yes. |

| PETER | For what reason? |

| RUTH | Just in case you wanted to visit. |

| PETER | Would you like me to visit? |

| RUTH | No. |

| PETER | Oh. |

| RUTH | I'd like you to come and live with me. |

| PETER | I thought you were leaving me. |

| RUTH | I had no intention of leaving you. |

| PETER | I'm sorry? |

| RUTH | It was a test. The final test. I wanted to see what would happen. |

PETER   And did I pass?

RUTH   We were both being tested.

PETER   Well did we both pass?

(Lights out. Lights up in house. SUSAN looks at RAY. Looks at the Babygrow.)

SUSAN   You know?

RAY   Yes.

SUSAN   How?

RAY   I overheard you talking to Rattenbury. And then I went to see your mother.

SUSAN   She didn't tell me.

RAY   I asked her not to. In fact I told her not to.

SUSAN   And how did she take that?

RAY   Pretty well. Given that I also told her that if she ever poked her nose into our business again she wouldn't be welcome in our house.

SUSAN   Ray!

RAY   She's an evil witch.

SUSAN   She's my mother. She just wants what's best for me.

RAY   She wants what's best for her, which is not to lose you. I'm not the enemy you know.

(Pause.)

RAY   Well? Are you going to make your choice?

(*A moment between them.* RAY *goes to the door. He opens it.*)

RAY   It's always the woman's choice so I understand.

SUSAN   And what would you choose?

RAY   I chose you – ten years ago. And I feel no different today than I did then.

(RAY *goes out through the door. Lights up on garden.* PETER *is standing by the hedge.* RUTH *some distance away.*)

PETER   Oh, hello.

RAY   Hello.

PETER   This is my wife, Ruth.

RAY   Hello.

RUTH   Yes, we spoke on the phone.

(SUSAN *comes out onto the patio. Pauses.*)

SUSAN   (*hard*) Don't just walk away from me.

RAY   I came out to get some air.

SUSAN   You always walk away from conflict.

RAY   I don't see any point in arguing. I've said all I have to say.

SUSAN   Have you? Well look at them.

(*She swings towards* PETER *and* RUTH.)

SUSAN   Look at them and find a point.

RAY	I'm not doing this now. You know how I feel. (*To* RUTH, *bitter*.) She's pregnant.
RUTH	Oh, how nice.
RAY	But she doesn't know if she wants to keep it. Her mother thinks it's a bad idea. (*To* SUSAN.) Doesn't she darling?
SUSAN	I'd rather not discuss this here, Ray.
RAY	Why not?
SUSAN	Because it's private.
RAY	Between you and me?
SUSAN	Yes.
RAY	So why get your mother involved?
SUSAN	(*to* PETER) This is your fault.
PETER	(*startled*) Is it?
SUSAN	Yes. If you'd just left when you were supposed to leave we wouldn't have got into this awful position.
RAY	Don't blame him.
SUSAN	Yes, well I'd expect you to take his side.
RAY	Maybe it's good that he stayed. Maybe it's brought things to a head.
RUTH	He does have a tendency of doing that.
PETER	Do I?

RUTH   Yes. I've always said it, haven't I? You like
              to get things sorted out. (*To* SUSAN.) He's a
              doer, very practical, you see. If there's a fuse
              to be mended, Peter will be there with his
              tool kit. If there's a crisis, he'll always offer
              a solution.

SUSAN   I can't bear this.

              (*She turns back towards the house. Stops.
              Turns to face them.*)

SUSAN   Ray?

RAY   What?

SUSAN   Will you come inside, please.

RAY   I'm perfectly happy out here thank you.

PETER   Should I fetch out another couple of deck
              chairs?

SUSAN   No! No you will not fetch out more deck
              chairs you stupid, stupid old man! Please,
              just go away and leave us alone! I mean
              for pity's sake, if nothing else you must be
              starving by now.

PETER   No. I'm fine thank you. The vegetable patch
              has been keeping me going.

SUSAN   You've been eating from the vegetable
              patch?

PETER   Yes.

SUSAN   Theft!

PETER   What?

SUSAN   I'm calling the police.

RUTH   I'm sure the police have enough on their
             plates, dear, without being alerted to the
             theft of a couple of radishes.

PETER   Spring onions and tomatoes, dear. I told you
             I didn't want to risk the radishes. I did have
             a few lettuces too.

RUTH   And how were they?

PETER   Very good, better than last year I think.

SUSAN   (*to* RUTH) It doesn't matter! It doesn't
             sodding matter what sodding vegetables they
             are. It's the principle. You're worse than he
             is, aren't you?

RUTH   Am I? In what respect?

SUSAN   You won't face up to anything! You talk and
             talk absolute rubbish, about anything, in
             fact, than the issue in question.

RUTH   I thought we were discussing salad. Weren't
             we discussing salad, darling?

PETER   Well I was.

SUSAN   And I wasn't! I was trying to discuss the
             issue of my pregnancy in the privacy of my
             garden with my husband. I really can't stand
             much more of this.

PETER   I'm sorry.

SUSAN   Are you really? And are you really qualified
             to get involved in a discussion about
             children given your track record?

RUTH   What?

                   (*A pause.* PETER *hangs his head.*)

SUSAN   Yes. Ray told me . . .

                   (*A look between* RAY *and* PETER.)

RAY   I'm sorry.

SUSAN   Stop apologizing to them. They should be
                   apologizing to us. (*To* RUTH.) Well? Is this
                   why you two talk about salad all day –
                   because you can't bear to discuss what really
                   matters?

RAY   That's enough.

SUSAN   Is it? I haven't even started yet.

                   (*She looks round the three of them.*)

SUSAN   I'm calling the police.

                   (*She goes into the house. A pause. The sound
                   of the commentary continues on the radio.*)

RAY   I'm sorry about that.

PETER   No. It's hardly your fault. I blame myself
                   entirely.

                   (*He looks at* RUTH.)

RUTH   Do you?

PETER   I wanted to protect you.

RUTH   I was more than capable of looking after
                   myself.

PETER	Nevertheless . . .

(RAY *moves away to give them some peace.*)

RUTH	Well? Is she right?
PETER	About?
RUTH	Us?
PETER	I don't think so. Do you think so?
RUTH	I'm not sure.

(*She goes towards the house. A wicket on the radio. Nobody acknowledges it. RUTH walks through the French doors into the house. PETER and RAY exchange a look. RAY shrugs.*)

PETER	I think children are . . . Necessary. Not vital. But necessary. Life is possible without them. Our life was . . . is . . .

(*He sits in the chair. His head drops a little. RAY goes over to him and puts a comforting hand on his shoulder. Lights out slowly. Lights up in house. SUSAN comes into the kitchen holding the cordless phone. RUTH is at the door.*)

RUTH	I promise I won't come any further in.
SUSAN	You might as well. The Police are on their way. They seem to think I have a strong case against your husband.
RUTH	I'm sure you have.

(RUTH *comes further in. Looks around.*)

RUTH   You've been busy.

SUSAN   Yes.

                (*A pause.*)

RUTH   You've taken the curtains down.

SUSAN   They went to the charity shop.

RUTH   Awful things. I don't know what I was
                thinking   . . . As soon as I put them up I
                knew they were wrong. But it seemed so
                wasteful to throw them away. So we lived
                with them. For nearly thirty years.

SUSAN   I'm not going to blame my hormones and
                I'm not going to apologize because . . .
                because to a large extent I meant what I said.
                But I'm sorry for the way I said it.

RUTH   Well I can't say it didn't hurt. But . . . I can
                understand why you're so upset.

                (SUSAN *looks round.*)

SUSAN   I wanted this house so much. (*To* RUTH.)
                You know? I thought, if we live here then
                everything will change. All the questions I
                have about everything will be answered by
                this house. It will give us a reason.

RUTH   Oh projects are vital. Moving house,
                curtains, cricket, crosswords . . . without
                them life is too empty.

SUSAN   And children?

RUTH   Another project. A more serious one, but
                a project nevertheless. Until they leave, I
                suspect, then one is left with oneself.

SUSAN   In some ways I envy you.

RUTH   Do you?

SUSAN   Yes. I saw the way you looked at one
               another.

RUTH   Oh, we're very fond of each other. But so
               are you and Ray. It's easy to be fond in
               old age when you no longer have all those
               troublesome urges and jealousies. You and
               Ray still have some fire, which is far more
               fun.

               (SUSAN *sits down.*)

SUSAN   I don't know what to do.

               (RUTH, *tentatively, sits too.*)

RUTH   About the child?

SUSAN   About anything.

RUTH   What would you do if you were alone?

SUSAN   Pregnant and alone?

RUTH   Yes.

SUSAN   Well I'd . . . Why do you ask that question?

RUTH   Because I want to know if the child is for
               you, or for you both. If this pregnancy is
               something designed simply to keep you
               together, then . . .

SUSAN   Then that's the wrong reason. Of course it is.
               I'm not stupid. We both went into this with
               our eyes open. We both so much wanted a
               child.

(RUTH *nods*.)

RUTH   But things have changed since then?

SUSAN   Yes. It's almost as if the thing we both
            wanted more than anything in the world has
            just . . . destroyed what was there before.
            What is it they say? Be careful of what you
            wish for in case it comes true.

RUTH   Is it that serious?

SUSAN   I don't know. I really don't know. Sometimes
            I think I hate him – really hate him. And
            then, ten minutes later, I look at him and
            I feel so much for him. Then he can say
            something that's just so stupid I want to hit
            him – and then . . . a moment later I feel
            sorry for him for having felt that way. Is that
            normal?

RUTH   Oh, quite normal. Men are ridiculous
            creatures. Look at Peter refusing to move
            out of the garden. I mean part of me admires
            him for it but the rest of me despairs that
            he couldn't do something recognizably
            normal – like booking into a hotel for a
            few days. That's why he stayed, you know.
            Not because he was making a stand – as
            he claimed – but because he simply didn't
            know how to go about finding a hotel and
            what he should do when he walked up to the
            reception desk. He'd deny it but believe me
            it's the absolute truth.

SUSAN   So what if you had had a son?

RUTH   Oh, I'd have schooled him much more
            effectively than Peter's mother. She was
            hopeless. Did everything for him and then
            just handed him on to me. He was like one
            of those demonstrator cars that garages sell.

Virtually new, but cheaper than a brand new car and not properly run in. That was Peter.

(*A pause.*)

And they were boys. The ones I lost. Both of them. The lost boys. But I'm a very good auntie. I hope.

SUSAN   I'm sure you are.

(*She goes to the window. Looks out. Lights up on garden. They stay up in house.* PETER *and* RAY *are in deck chairs, side by side, listening to the test.*)

RUTH   I'm sure you'll make the right choice.

(SUSAN *remains looking out of the window.* RUTH *goes out into the garden.*)

PETER   All done?

RUTH   Yes. How are they doing?

(RAY *stands, then passes her – they exchange a glance – he then goes in through the French doors.*)

PETER   They've staged a recovery but I think we're aiming for a draw.

RUTH   What a terrible waste of five days.

PETER   Oh, it wasn't a waste at all. The result is not everything. It's how you achieve it. That's the most important thing.

RUTH   What were you two discussing?

PETER	If you really must know, we were discussing whether to set up house together and leave you two to get on with it.
RUTH	And you decided against it?
PETER	Yes. On the grounds that Ray said he didn't want people thinking he was my Toy Boy – whatever one of those is.
RUTH	Well?
PETER	Well what?
RUTH	Are you coming?
PETER	. . . No.
RUTH	No?
PETER	No. I'm not coming. I've never been to Bexhill-on-Sea. I might not like it.
RUTH	Oh. I see.
PETER	Good. Because I've been doing some thinking too – and I can't say that I'm particularly happy that you sold the house without consulting me.
RUTH	It had to be done.
PETER	Well I beg to differ on that one. So I will come and visit you, Ruth. And then I will make my decision.
RUTH	That's very kind of you . . . And where will you stay until then?
PETER	In a hotel. With room service. And a television – and tea-making facilities.

RUTH	And how will you go about booking it?
PETER	I've already done it. Ray did it with his phone. It's called a Blueberry. It's marvellous – you can virtually run your life with it without leaving your deck chair. I may well get one.
RUTH	Right then.
PETER	Right.
RUTH	Well, goodbye then.
PETER	Goodbye.

(*She goes to the gate and pauses*.)

RUTH	Do let me know where you're staying.
PETER	I will. I'll text you from my new telephone.
RUTH	Thank you. You do have my number?
PETER	Yes. I do.
RUTH	And you're intending buying a new phone soon?
PETER	I am.

(*Pause*.)

RUTH	I should have thrown those curtains away the moment I put them up. But we made do, didn't we?

(*She turns and walks away. The lights go up in the house.* PETER *stands and begins to pack his things into his case.* RAY *is watching from the window*.)

RAY   Susan. (*Pause.*) Susan.

SUSAN   (*off*) What?

RAY   Come here.

               (SUSAN *comes to join him at the window.*
               PETER, *having packed, carries his cases to
               the gate. He turns to look back at the house.
               He sees* RAY *at the window.* PETER *nods.* RAY
               nods back. Smiles. PETER *exits through the
               garden gate.*)

RAY   Gone.

SUSAN   About time. She must have talked him round.

RAY   He's not so bad, you know.

SUSAN   Let's not go through all that again.

RAY   So?

               (*He looks at the Babygrow.* SUSAN *does too.
               Then she leaves the room and emerges into
               the garden.* RAY *follows her out. She stands
               in the centre of the lawn. It's her territory
               now.*)

SUSAN   . . . When you said we might bump into each
               other in the street in forty years' time . . .

RAY   Yes?

SUSAN   I had a terrible cold feeling. A terrible
               feeling of loss.

               (*They look at each other.*)

SUSAN   Now he's gone, can we start again?

RAY   Just pretend he was never here?

SUSAN   No. Remember he was here – and remember why.

             (*She looks around the garden.*)

SUSAN   We can be happy here.

RAY   Can we?

             (*She holds out her hand.* RAY *approaches her. She takes* RAY'S *hand.*)

SUSAN   Yes.

             (*She guides his hand to her stomach and covers it with hers. Slow fade to black.*)